The Life of an Intercessor

TEACH US HOW TO PRAY
PRAYER JOURNAL

TIFFANY THOMPSON

McClure Publishing, Inc.

"The Life of an Intercessor"
Never ever underestimate the power of intercessory prayer

An Intercessor:

Someone who intervenes on behalf of another, an Advocate, especially by prayer.

The Life of an Intercessor - Copyright © 2017

All rights reserved. Printed and bound in the United States of America. According to the 1976 United States Copyright Act, no part of this book may be reproduced or utilized in any form or by any means, electronic or mechanical, including photocopying, recording, or by any information storage or retrieval system, except by a reviewer who may quote brief passages in a review to be printed in a magazine or newspaper, without permission in writing from the Publisher: Inquiries should be addressed to McClure Publishing, Inc. Permissions Department, 398 West Army Trail Road, Suite 124, Bloomingdale, Illinois 60108. Publication date: **July 17, 2017**.

The author and publisher have made every effort to ensure the accuracy and completeness of information contained in this book. We assume no responsibility for errors, inaccuracies, omissions, or any inconsistencies therein.

New International Version (NIV) Holy Bible, New International Version®, NIV® Copyright ©1973, 1978, 1984, 2011 by Biblica, Inc.® Used by permission. All rights reserved worldwide.

Scriptures marked KJV are taken from the KING JAMES VERSION (KJV): KING JAMES VERSION, public domain.

Amplified Bible (AMP) Copyright © 2015 by The Lockman Foundation, La Habra, CA 90631. All rights reserved.

New Living Translation (NLT) *Holy Bible,* New Living Translation, copyright © 1996, 2004, 2015 by Tyndale House Foundation. Used by permission of Tyndale House Publishers Inc., Carol Stream, Illinois 60188. All rights reserved.

New King James Version (NKJV) Scripture taken from the New King James Version®. Copyright © 1982 by Thomas Nelson. Used by permission. All rights reserved.

New American Standard Bible (NASB) Copyright © 1960, 1962, 1963, 1968, 1971, 1972, 1973, 1975, 1977, 1995 by The Lockman Foundation

ISBN 13: 978-0-9989223-9-3

Cover Design by Dr. Bernice McCoy
Author's photo by Dyron Bailey

Interior layout by Kathy McClure
To order additional copies,
log on to: https://www.mcclurepublishing.com

DEDICATION

This book is dedicated to all Intercessors and all up and rising Intercessors.

50 Intercessory Prayer Topics

Page

1. Intercessors forgive quickly 21
2. Intercessors' ears are attentive 22
3. Intercessors know the voice of God 23
4. Intercessors are brave 24
5. Intercessors pray the word 25
6. Intercessors are trustworthy 26
7. Intercessors do not gossip 27
8. Intercessors train other intercessors 28
9. Intercessors are warriors 29
10. Intercessors will stand alone 30
11. Intercessors run to and not from 31
12. Intercessors are humble 32
13. Intercessors are strategic 33
14. Intercessors love hard 34
15. Intercessors are worshippers 35
16. Intercessors take hits 36
17. Intercessors are on the front line 37
18. Intercessors go to battle 38
19. Intercessors discern different spirits 39
20. Intercessors are skilled and trained warriors 40
21. Intercessors are full of wisdom 41
22. Intercessors carry favor 42
23. Intercessors keep the sword in their hand and mouth 43
24. Intercessors forsake themselves 44

25.	Intercessors pray for their enemies	45
26.	Intercessors say what God says	46
27.	Intercessors expect miracles	47
28.	Intercessors encourage themselves	48
29.	Intercessors are accountable	49
30.	Intercessors activate	50
31.	Intercessors are midwives	51
32.	Intercessors build one another	52
33.	Intercessors sing to the Lord	53
34.	Intercessors walk in integrity	54
35.	Intercessors speak life	55
36.	Intercessors resurrect	56
37.	Intercessors carry the glory	57
38.	Intercessors go through periods of crushing	58
39.	Intercessors are oracles of God	59
40.	Intercessors are watchmen	60
41.	Intercessors are planted	61
42.	Intercessors walk in agreement with God	62
43.	Intercessors walk by faith	63
44.	Intercessors hate what God hates	64
45.	Intercessors obey God	65
46.	Intercessors make declarations	66
47.	Intercessors destroy the plans of hell	67
48.	Intercessors have access to heaven	68
49.	Intercessors rebuke and correct	69
50.	Intercessors are submissive	70

"LORD TEACH US HOW TO PRAY"

> *And it came to pass, that, as he was praying in a certain place, when he ceased, one of his disciples said unto him, Lord, teach us to pray, as John also taught his disciples.*

Luke 11:1 (KJV)

I believe Jesus stirred up a hunger in the particular disciple as he sat back and watched Jesus praying. He had a desire, a yearning to do what he saw. Jesus was not the only templet but John was as well, because he said teach us just like John also taught his disciples.

The more we set an example, the more people will desire and crave what they see. I feel like this disciple felt a burden to pray but did not know how, so he asked Jesus to teach them all how to PRAY.

THE LIFE OF AN INTERCESSOR

"LORD TEACH US HOW TO PRAY"

INTRODUCTION

I was burden by the Lord to write and give information to what an intercessor is and what this office holds. Many times we are not aware of what our position is with God when we are unaware of our identity in Him. Until then, we will never believe that He hears us and we will continue to walk in life feeling defeated.

What I believe God wants us all to know is that we are all called to intercession. It's not only the pastors' job at the church to pray, but everyone is assigned to pray, talk with, and listen to God.

Prayer is having a conversation, communing, listening and walking with God who is our Father. I believe one of the biggest problems is we think that if we are not in a church building, we are not qualified to communicate with the Father.

A relationship with Jesus Christ is the first relationship we should seek after. Up until the time we realize we need Him, we will remain lost and powerless. Once we recognize that He is our only source of power, we will see how much we really need Him.

I can remember when I first received Jesus as my Lord and Savior in 2004, that I realized I really needed Him. I felt so out of place and the adversary (the devil) made sure he kept me in that place. Going over and over in mind was that *you were not raised in the church; you are not fluent in the things of God.* Visiting every now and again with friends and neighbors, did not help, so when I gave my life to Christ, I truly realized how lost I was.

A friend of mine who was already saved, told me about a church on the west side of Chicago that was having prayer every Tuesday afternoon. She was very excited about going to prayer on Tuesdays. I did not quite understand what the big deal was all about. I felt the exact same way about attending church. It was all foreign to me. I knew more about Ice Cube, 50 Cent, Jay Z, Tupac, Biggy, etc....

She began to name names such as Juanita Bynum, Mother Katherine Bynum and so on and so forth. I am looking at her thinking, *so what. Who are these people? I do not know any of them and they do not know me. I don't belong here, because I'm a sinner deep in sin and there is no way or no one who can save a wretch like me.*

I always told myself, when I turned a certain age; this is how I am going to die! Everything else is a fairytale, these people are known on television, and I am known on the block. But because she did not have a car anymore, she needed a ride and I thought to myself, *this is the least that I can do and that is to give her a ride to church.* She is the only one that I am aware of in the neighborhood that has made a change so let me support her.

All along God was setting me up to get in His presence and transform my life from what I was around. I knew that the people I was around in the world was really shaping my life and dictating my future.

When I first walked in the door, I began looking around at how everyone was really super-charged about getting together. She introduced me to several people then the prayer service started. It blew my mind how the presence of God filled that place. Before I knew it, I had entered into a different place. It was life changing. I knew then that this is what I needed to transform me into my purpose and the reason why I exist.

I decided to continue taking her to prayer. Besides the Lord was breaking up all my fake friendships and relationships, so I pretty much had nothing left to look forward to. And, yes, it was frustrating and hurtful, and that was only because just like any other human, I did not understand what was going on. I had already lost the majority of everyone I loved.

As I continued going each time, sitting in the church feeling lost and like a misfit. They spoke all kinds of different languages that I did not understand. People were screaming and hollering as they were being delivered from demonic influence. I witnessed demons being cast out. I thought to myself, *I better get out of here. This isn't for me and it's spooky.*

The reason I am giving you my foundation is because you probably feel or have felt just like me in the beginning. Church members would prophecy to me, though I did not know what they were doing at the time. I lacked understanding but all I knew is that I wanted to be saved. They imparted words of love and spoke life unto me. These words counterattacked what I received from the world, which was hate and death. This is all I knew. In all honesty they had lots and lots of work to do on me. Because of the Spirit of Intercession, they were patient with me and their labor was not in vain. They prayed for me until the chains of bondage were broken. I felt like a new woman. The heavy weights that were upon me, lifted off me and I became a better person.

I continued going and joined the ministry. Everything began to grow on me. In other words, my new circle/church family began to shape my new world and my new future.

I would like to encourage you to never believe that you are too far or too deep involved that the Father cannot reach you. Do not ever feel that you have no place in the Kingdom of God because He always has room for His Intercessors.

Now, just because I used the word Intercessor does not exclude you because anyone who is living with breath in their body, is called to intercede and pray for someone even if it's for children, our neighbors, or our president. We all need to have an open line of communication with God.

My advice is to allow the teaching and the leading of God and your leaders to cultivate and develop the intercessor in you so that you can effectively pray for the Glory of God.

I can remember being so ready to jump right in and get on the front line not knowing the devil had a kingdom and demons are enlisted in different ranks just like the Kingdom of God. So, please take your time and learn to study the Word of God and receive as much training as possible. Be anxious for nothing but in everything pray. As you are being led by God, He will guide and lead you in prayer.

The majority of my prayer life happened at home. My prayer life started with interceding for myself, my husband, children and family before God had me pray for others.

I would like to share a few scriptures to build your confidence in praying to God, remember just because you are called to intercede does not mean that life will be *smooth sailing*. There will be times when you are strong and there will be times when you are weak. While Paul is teaching in Corinth, he explains a conversation he is having with Christ which helped him draw a conclusion,

But He said to me, "My grace is sufficient for you, for my power is made perfect in weakness." Therefore I will boast all the more gladly about my weaknesses, so that Christ's power may rest on me.

(2 Corinthians 12:9 - NIV)

Being weak and being strong in the Lord either way we still win because Jesus chose us and we received and accepted the call. We will not ever be defeated despite what the flesh feels. The only time defeat comes in and win is when we move in our own strength and not in the strength of God.

I John 5:14 (NIV)

This is the confidence we have in approaching God: that if we ask anything according to His will, he hears us.

This is a scripture of confidence because I know that if I ask anything in prayer according to the will of God which is His word, He hears me.

This is letting us know that we do not have to second guess God just because we are not perfect. The thing is we were not perfect when He called us out of bars, the clubs, off drugs, from sin, etc.... What we are doing today as we live in Him and seek Him the more, we are daily striving towards perfection, and we cannot do it outside of Him.

God does not want us to run away from Him when things are not going the way we believe they should go. He would rather that we run towards Him in prayer. Here is another scripture that would encourage you that God desires us to pray to Him.

Ezekiel 22:30 (NIV)

I looked for someone among them who would build up the wall and stand before me in the gap on behalf of the land so I would not have to destroy it, but I found no one.

This is the heart of God speaking to Ezekiel. He did not say that He was looking for someone who had it all together. He is looking for someone that will accept the call to intercede, someone who would just say, yes, and make themselves available so that He would not have to destroy the people.

St. John 11:42 (NLT)

You always hear me, but I said it out loud for the sake of all these people standing here, so that they will believe you sent me.

This is Jesus praying to God in the presence of all the people. He spoke in confidence. He did it openly to build the faith of those that were around, imparting hope at the same time while performing a miracle. He was the first example.

Hebrews 11:6 (NIV)

And without faith it is impossible to please God, because anyone who comes to Him must believe that He exists and that he rewards those who earnestly seek Him.

This is another example of scripture that exemplify God moving in the miraculous, by Faith. We have to believe that He even exists. The question is if God is real? Then the next step of faith is knowing that He is going to reward us in whatever area He decides to reward us because we seek Him.

Romans 8:26 (NIV)

In the same way, the Spirit helps us in our weakness. We do not know what we ought to pray for, but the Spirit himself intercedes for us through wordless groans.

As you can see this scripture helps build all of our confidence in the Lord. It is the Spirit of the Lord that gives us what to pray. How do we do that? We humble ourselves before Him and ask the Father to give us direction and guidance for what is on His heart.

Develop an intimate relationship with God, so that you can pray as He leads.

PERSONAL AND CORPORATE INTERCESSION

God speaks to us through our senses. We may hear His voice audibly or through our spirit, we may feel a certain pain, we may see a glimpse of a vision that He wants us to pray for, and/or Holy Spirit will pray through us with words that cannot be uttered. However, God wants to move during our time of intercession, allow Him.

Do not box God in. He may speak to us differently during prayer. Never expect Him to move the exact same way each and every time. Be open to allowing Him access to use you as a catalyst. When we allow God to move during intercessory prayer, we may pray out loud or silently, we may moan during our time of intercession, we may pray in an unknown tongue, we may war or pray prophetically, we may sing a song to the Lord, and He may sing a song back to us. Remember this is not the time to show case that you are gifted. Let God use you and surrender to the leading of Holy Spirit.

An intercessor studies the word of God to use as a mighty battle-axe against the enemy. An intercessor studies the word of God to remind God what His word says, although, He already knows. An intercessor studies the word of God so that Holy Spirit can bring it to our remembrance. God speaks to us through His word. An intercessor may also enter into someone's pain/suffering in order to take it to the

Lord. An intercessor prays from a heavenly perspective that the prayer has already been answered.

In corporate intercession, a lead intercessor must be chosen to give direction of the prayers going forth. Always remain humble and submissive. It is through tag teaming that keeps the flow of the Spirit of God moving during corporate intercession. All the team members may speak in an unknown tongue corporately to usher in the presence of God. Remove spirits of pride, envy, jealousy, and the like. Release love, joy, and peace. Those who do not speak in an unknown tongue please do not let that hinder the Spirit of the Lord moving through you. We can get caught up in formalities that we miss the move of God, so be led by His Spirit.

When praying with others, each person may receive something different. This does not mean that you or they are not hearing from God concerning what to pray for. Everyone has a gift that may or may not be similar to others but it is the same Spirit.

By: *Dr. Kathy McClure*

1. Intercessors forgive quickly

Scripture: Colossians 3:13 (AMP)
bearing graciously with one another, and willingly forgiving each other if one has a cause for complaint against another; just as the Lord has forgiven you, so should you forgive.

Prayer:

Lord, God, we thank You because you made us in your image after your likeness. We have the power to forgive completely and quickly as you have forgiven us, in Jesus' name. Amen.

"Write out your prayer pertaining to the above scripture." _____

_____
_____
_____
_____
_____

2. Intercessors' ears are attentive

Scripture: Psalm 34:15 (NIV)
The eyes of the Lord are on the righteous, and His ears are attentive to their cry;

Prayer:

Lord, thank You that Your eyes are everywhere and Your ears are attentive to our prayers. We understand that You are against those that do evil, and we thank You for defending us, in Jesus' name. Amen.

"Write out your prayer pertaining to the above scripture." _____

_____
_____
_____
_____
_____
_____
_____
_____

3. Intercessors know the voice of God

Scripture: Romans 8:26 (NIV)
In the same way, the Spirit helps us in our weakness. We do not know what we ought to pray for, but the Spirit himself intercedes for us through wordless groans.

Prayer:

Lord, thank You for Your spirit. Thank You for helping us with our weaknesses and teaching us the things to pray for. God, I thank You for being my ultimate intercessor, in Jesus' name. Amen.

"Write out your prayer pertaining to the above scripture." _____
_____
_____
_____
_____
_____

4. Intercessors are brave

Scripture: Joshua 1:9 (NIV)
Have I not commanded you? Be strong and courageous. Do not be afraid; do not be discouraged, for the LORD your God will be with you wherever you go."

Prayer:

Thank You, God, that You are the one that made me strong and courageous in You. It's because of You that I do not fear, and I will not be discouraged. I believe that You are everywhere I go in, Jesus' name. Amen.

"Write out your prayer pertaining to the above scripture." _____

_____
_____
_____
_____
_____

5. Intercessors pray the word

Scripture: Hebrews 4:12 (NIV)
For the word of God is alive and active. Sharper than any double-edged sword, it penetrates even to dividing soul and spirit, joints and marrow; it judges the thoughts and attitudes of the heart.

Prayer:

Thank You, God, that Your word is sharper than a double edge sword. Thank You, God that I can speak the word and You will respond quickly. Thank You, Lord that Your word is the ultimate judge, in Jesus' name. Amen.

"Write out your prayer pertaining to the above scripture." _____
_____
_____
_____
_____

6. Intercessors are trustworthy

Scripture: 1 Thessalonians 2:4 (NIV)
On the contrary, we speak as those approved by God to be entrusted with the gospel. We are not trying to please people but God, who tests our hearts.

Prayer:

Thank You, God, for entrusting me with the Gospel of Christ. Thank You for teaching me to please You and not man. Thank You for approving and testing my heart, in Jesus' name. Amen.

"Write out your prayer pertaining to the above scripture." _____
_____
_____
_____
_____
_____

7. Intercessors do not gossip

Scripture: James 3:5 (NIV)
Likewise, the tongue is a small part of the body, but it makes great boasts. Consider what a great forest is set on fire by a small spark.

Prayer:

Thank You, God, for my tongue that I will use to bless and not curse. I will use it to uplift and not degrade, in Jesus' name. Amen.

"Write out your prayer pertaining to the above scripture." _____

_____
_____
_____
_____
_____
_____
_____

8. Intercessors train other intercessors

Scripture: Titus 2:3 (NIV)
Likewise, teach the older women to be reverent in the way they live, not to be slanderers or addicted to much wine, but to teach what is good.

Prayer:

Thank You, God, for developing me to be a teacher of Your word and not to be a slanderer and an overcomer of addictions, in the name of Yeshua. Amen.

"Write out your prayer pertaining to the above scripture." _____

_____
_____
_____
_____
_____

9. Intercessors are warriors

Scripture: Psalm 144:1 (NIV)
Praise be to the Lord my Rock, who trains my hands for war, my fingers for battle.

Prayer:

Thank You, God that you have trained my hands for spiritual war and my fingers to fight and because of that I have the victory, in Jesus' name. Amen.

"Write out your prayer pertaining to the above scripture." _____

_____
_____
_____
_____
_____
_____
_____
_____
_____

10. Intercessors will stand alone

Scripture: 1 Samuel 30:6 (KJV)
And David was greatly distressed; f or the people spake of stoning him, because the soul of all the people was grieved, every man for his sons and for his daughters: but David encouraged himself in the LORD his God.

Prayer:

Thank You, Lord that because of You I can stand against anything, even when my enemies stand against me. I will stand on Your word and encourage myself, in the name of Jesus. Amen.

"Write out your prayer pertaining to the above scripture." _____
_____
_____
_____
_____

11. Intercessors run to and not from

Scripture: Isaiah 40:31 (NIV)
but those who hope in the LORD will renew their strength. They will soar on wings like eagles; they will run and not grow weary, they will walk and not be faint.

Prayer:

Thank You, Lord, for the strength to run and not grow weary. Lord, it is because of You that I can soar with wings like eagles and not faint when I am faced with all sorts of obstacles, in Jesus' name. Amen.

"Write out your prayer pertaining to the above scripture." _____

_____
_____
_____
_____
_____

12. Intercessors are humble

Scripture: James 4:10 (NIV)
Humble yourselves before the Lord, and he will lift you up.

Prayer:

Thank You, God, for giving me instructions to humble myself and, therefore, You do not have to. I thank God for allowing humility to be my posture before You and man, in Jesus' name, Amen.

"Write out your prayer pertaining to the above scripture." _____

_____
_____
_____
_____
_____
_____
_____
_____

13. Intercessors are strategic

Scripture: Jeremiah 9:17 (KJV)
Thus saith the Lord of hosts, Consider ye, and call for the mourning women, that they may come; and send for cunning women, that they may come:

Prayer:

Thank You, God, for Your wisdom and understanding that we may know what to pray in season and out of season. Lord, continue to teach us how to moan and wail on behalf of Your people, in Jesus' name. Amen.

"Write out your prayer pertaining to the above scripture." _____

_____
_____
_____
_____
_____
_____

14. Intercessors love hard

Scripture: 2 Samuel 1:26 (NIV)

I grieve for you, Jonathan my brother; you were very dear to me. Your love for me was wonderful, more wonderful than that of women.

Prayer:

Thank You, God, for teaching us how to love, the meaning of love and what love is. It is unconditional (agape). I pray that the hearts of all intercessors would have this same love, in the name of Yeshua. Amen.

"Write out your prayer pertaining to the above scripture." _____

_____
_____
_____
_____
_____
_____

15. Intercessors are worshippers

Scripture: 2 Samuel 6:14 (NIV)
Wearing a linen ephod, David was dancing before the LORD with all his might,

Prayer:

Thank You, God, for allowing our feet to dance before thee and thee only. We shall continue to dance in Your presence wearing priestly garments before You, Lord, in Jesus' name Amen.

"Write out your prayer pertaining to the above scripture." _____
_____
_____
_____
_____
_____
_____
_____

16. Intercessors take hits

Scripture: Psalm 23:3 (NKJV)
He restores my soul; He leads me in the paths of righteousness For His name's sake.

Prayer:

Thank You, God, for being here for me in spite of all that I have been through. You are truly the one who restores my soul and leads me in the path of righteousness for Your name sake. I just want to thank You for being that good to me, in Jesus' name, Amen.

"Write out your prayer pertaining to the above scripture." _____
_____
_____
_____
_____
_____
_____
_____

17. Intercessors are on the front line

Scripture: 2 Chronicles 20:1 (KJV)
It came to pass after this also, that the children of Moab, and the children of Ammon, and with them other beside the Ammonites, came against Jehoshaphat to battle.

Prayer:

Thank You, God, that as an intercessor, I understand that I may have to go first, but I understand and know that even as I stand on the frontline, God, You are there with me despite what and who comes up against me, in Jesus' name Amen.

"Write out your prayer pertaining to the above scripture." _____
_____
_____
_____
_____

18. Intercessors go to battle

Scripture: 1 Samuel 30:8 (NIV)
and David inquired of the LORD, "Shall I pursue this raiding party? Will I overtake them?"

"Pursue them," he answered. "You will certainly overtake them and succeed in the rescue."

Prayer:

Thank You, God that You are the one who leads us even in battle. God, You are great and full of wisdom that is why we seek You and only You before pursuing our enemies, in the name of Yeshua. Amen.

"Write out your prayer pertaining to the above scripture." _____

_____
_____
_____
_____
_____

19. Intercessors discern different spirits

Scripture: 1 Corinthians 12:10 (KJV)
To another the working of miracles; to another prophecy; to another discerning of spirits; to another divers kinds of tongues; to another the interpretation of tongues:

Prayer:

Thank You, God, for Your wonderful gifts that You have given me to help locate agents in my soul, to bring healing and deliverance to Your people, in the name of Yeshua. Amen.

"Write out your prayer pertaining to the above scripture." _____
_____
_____
_____
_____
_____

20. Intercessors are skilled and trained warriors

Scripture: 1 Chronicles 12:1-2 (NLT)

The following men joined David at Ziklag while he was hiding from Saul son of Kish. They were among the warriors who fought beside David in battle. ²All of them were expert archers, and they could shoot arrows or sling stones with their left hand as well as their right. They were all relatives of Saul from the tribe of Benjamin.

Prayer:

Thank You, God, for instilling inside of me the gift of the trained one. Lord, thank You for cultivating and developing me for hard times and for times of war, in the name of Jesus. Amen.

"Write out your prayer pertaining to the above scripture." _____
_____
_____

21. Intercessors are full of wisdom

Scripture: Luke 7:35 (NIV)
But wisdom is proved right by all her children.

Prayer:

Thank You, God, for filling me with your awesome wisdom and power. I am forever grateful to be identified by wisdom. Because of wisdom, I know how to respond, in Jesus' name. Amen.

"Write out your prayer pertaining to the above scripture." _____
_____
_____
_____
_____
_____
_____
_____
_____
_____

22. Intercessors carry favor

Scripture: Psalm 30:5 (KJV)
> *For his anger endureth but a moment; in his favour is life: weeping may endure for a night, but joy cometh in the morning.*

Prayer:

Thank You, God, for Your extended favor with You first and then man. Thank You, God that Your favor gives me access to things that I do not qualify for. Your favor is for a lifetime and not temporary, in the name of Jesus. Amen.

"Write out your prayer pertaining to the above scripture." _____
_____
_____
_____
_____
_____
_____

23. Intercessors keep the sword in their hand and mouth

Scripture: Psalm 144:1 (NIV)
Praise be to the LORD my Rock, who trains my hands for war, my fingers for battle.

Prayer:

Thank You, Lord, for training me. Lord, You are my Rock and you have never lost a battle and because of You, I win, in Jesus' Name. Amen.

"Write out your prayer pertaining to the above scripture." _____
_____
_____
_____
_____
_____
_____
_____
_____

24. Intercessors forsake themselves

Scripture: Hebrews 10:25 (NIV)
not giving up meeting together, as some are in the habit of doing, but encouraging one another—and all the more as you see the Day approaching.

Prayer:

Thank You, Lord, for giving us the wisdom and the love knowing that we should continue to encourage each other daily as you see fit, in Jesus' Name. Amen.

"Write out your prayer pertaining to the above scripture." _____

_____
_____
_____
_____
_____
_____
_____

25. Intercessors pray for their enemies

Scripture: Matthew 5:44 (NIV)
But I tell you, love your enemies and pray for those who persecute you,

Prayer:

Thank You, Lord, for the love that I have for my enemies and the intercession that is down in me for those who persecute me for Your name sake, in Jesus' Name. Amen.

"Write out your prayer pertaining to the above scripture." _____

_____
_____
_____
_____
_____
_____
_____
_____
_____

26. Intercessors say what God says

Scripture: John 5:19 (NIV)
Jesus gave them this answer: "Very truly I tell you, the Son can do nothing by himself; he can do only what he sees his Father doing, because whatever the Father does the Son also does.

Prayer:

Thank You, God, for being the ultimate intercessor in our lives, we do not know what to pray as we ought but because of our relationship with You, we pray what you say, in the name of Jesus. Amen.

"Write out your prayer pertaining to the above scripture." _____
_____
_____
_____
_____

27. Intercessors expect miracles

Scripture: Mark 16:17 (NIV)
And these signs will accompany those who believe: In my name they will drive out demons; they will speak in new tongues;

Prayer:

Thank You, Lord, for Your signs and wonders that follow me and because I believe, I have power to drive out devils and speak in new tongues, in Jesus Name. Amen.

"Write out your prayer pertaining to the above scripture." _____

_____
_____
_____
_____
_____
_____
_____
_____

28. Intercessors encourage themselves

Scripture: 1 Samuel 30:6 (NIV)
David was greatly distressed because the men were talking of stoning him; each one was bitter in spirit because of his sons and daughters. But David found strength in the LORD his God.

Prayer:

Thank You, Lord, just like Your son, David, when people are acting indifferent toward us, we can do just like him and find all of our strength in You, in Jesus' Name. Amen.

"Write out your prayer pertaining to the above scripture." _____

_____
_____
_____
_____
_____

29. Intercessors are accountable

Scripture: Romans 14:12 (NASB)
So then each one of us will give an account of himself to God.

Prayer:

Thank You, Lord that I understand that when it's all said and done, I have to give an account of myself to You and then man in Jesus' name. Amen.

"Write out your prayer pertaining to the above scripture." _____

_____
_____
_____
_____
_____
_____
_____
_____
_____

30. Intercessors activate

Scripture: Luke 11:1 (NIV)
One day Jesus was praying in a certain place. When he finished, one of his disciples said to him, "Lord, teach us to pray, just as John taught his disciples."

Prayer:

Thank You, Lord, for your many activations. Nevertheless, the one that is so dear to You is having direct communication with You, God. Continue to teach us how to pray as You have taught Your disciples that went before us, in Jesus' name. Amen.

"Write out your prayer pertaining to the above scripture." _____

_____
_____
_____
_____
_____

31. Intercessors are midwives

Scripture: Exodus 1:17 (NIV)
The midwives, however, feared God and did not do what the king of Egypt had told them to do; they let the boys live.

Prayer:

Thank You, Lord that we don't have to fear man and our godly reverence and obedience is in You, in Jesus' name. Amen.

"Write out your prayer pertaining to the above scripture." _____

_____
_____
_____
_____
_____
_____
_____
_____
_____

32. Intercessors build one another

Scripture: 1 Thessalonians 5:11 (NIV)
Therefore encourage one another and build each other up, just as in fact you are doing.

Prayer:

Thank You, Lord, for empowering us with Your love that we may love one another and build up each other according to Your will and Your word, in Jesus' name. Amen.

"Write out your prayer pertaining to the above scripture." _____

_____
_____
_____
_____
_____
_____
_____
_____
_____

33. Intercessors sing to the Lord

Scripture: 2 Samuel 22:1 (NIV)
David sang to the Lord the words of this song when the Lord delivered him from the hand of all his enemies and from the hand of Saul.

Prayer:

Thank You, Lord, for giving me a new song to express to You how thankful I am for You delivering me out the hands of my enemies, in Jesus' name. Amen.

"Write out your prayer pertaining to the above scripture." _____

_____
_____
_____
_____
_____
_____
_____

34. Intercessors walk in integrity

Scripture: 1 Peter 3:16 (NIV)
keeping a clear conscience, so that those who speak maliciously against your good behavior in Christ may be ashamed of their slander.

Prayer:

Thank You, Lord, for giving me a clear conscience and a clean record to walk before You in integrity; therefore, when man speaks maliciously against me, I will not be ashamed, in Jesus' name. Amen.

"Write out your prayer pertaining to the above scripture." _____

_____
_____
_____
_____
_____
_____

35. Intercessors speak life

Scripture: John 6:63 (NIV)
The Spirit gives life; the flesh counts for nothing. The words I have spoken to you—they are full of the Spirit and life.

Prayer:

Thank You, Lord God that I am able to speak words that are full of the spirit and life. I now understand that in my old nature the things of the flesh counted for nothing. Thank you for restoring me back to You, in Jesus' name. Amen.

"Write out your prayer pertaining to the above scripture." _____

_____
_____
_____
_____
_____
_____

36. Intercessors resurrect

Scripture: Philippians 3:10 (NIV)
I want to know Christ—yes, to know the power of his resurrection and participation in his sufferings, becoming like him in his death,

Prayer:

Thank You, Lord, for a deeper relationship and a desire to know Your power and a willingness to participate in Your sufferings, becoming more and more like You, in Jesus' name. Amen.

"Write out your prayer pertaining to the above scripture." _____

_____
_____
_____
_____
_____
_____

37. Intercessors carry the glory

Scripture: Exodus 33:15 (NIV)
Then Moses said to him, "If your Presence does not go with us, do not send us up from here.

Prayer:

Thank you Lord for your Glory, we declare to be a people that do not want to go if your glory is not going with us in Jesus Name. Amen.

"Write out your prayer pertaining to the above scripture." _____
_____
_____
_____
_____
_____
_____
_____
_____
_____

38. Intercessors go through periods of crushing

Scripture: Isaiah 53:10 (NIV)
> *Yet it was the LORD's will to crush him and cause him to suffer, and though he LORD makes his life an offering for sin, he will see his offspring and prolong his days, and the will of the LORD will prosper in his hand.*

Prayer:

Thank You, Lord God, for choosing us the way You chose and sent your Son to die for You. Your word declares that it was Your will to crush Him and to cause Him to suffer. Lord, we only want Your crushing and what is going to bring You glory in our lives, in Jesus' name. Amen.

"Write out your prayer pertaining to the above scripture." _____

_____
_____
_____

39. Intercessors are oracles of God

Scripture: 1 Peter 4:11 (NIV)
If anyone speaks, they should do so as one who speaks the very words of God. If anyone serves, they should do so with the strength God provides, so that in all things God may be praised through Jesus Christ. To him be the glory and the power for ever and ever. Amen.

Prayer:

Thank You, Lord, for giving me access and authority to Your word. God I will do and speak as a catalyst and Your Oracle as if I am serving You and only You, in Jesus name. Amen.

"Write out your prayer pertaining to the above scripture." _____

_____
_____
_____

40. Intercessors are watchmen

Scripture: Ezekiel 33:7 (NIV)
"Son of man, I have made you a watchman for the people of Israel; so hear the word I speak and give them warning from me.

Prayer:

Thank You, Lord that you have made my voice as a trumpet to hear what You speak and give warning to the people of God, in Jesus' name. Amen.

"Write out your prayer pertaining to the above scripture." _____

_____
_____
_____
_____
_____
_____
_____
_____

41. Intercessors are planted

Scripture: Psalm 1:3 (NIV)
That person is like a tree planted by streams of water, which yields its fruit in season and whose leaf does not wither— whatever they do prospers.

Prayer:

Thank You, Lord God, for being rooted and grounded in You. Your word says, I shall be like a tree planted by streams of water which I know God's water gives life and keeps me alive in You, in Jesus' name. Amen.

"Write out your prayer pertaining to the above scripture." _____

_____
_____
_____
_____
_____
_____

42. Intercessors walk in agreement with God

Scripture: Matthew 18:20 (NIV)
For where two or three gather in my name, there am I with them."

Prayer:

Thank You, Lord that when I pray or communicate in agreement with another sister or brother, You are there with us and for that we say thank You the more, in Jesus' name. Amen.

"Write out your prayer pertaining to the above scripture." _____

_____
_____
_____
_____
_____
_____
_____
_____

43. Intercessors walk by faith

Scripture: Hebrews 11:6 (NIV)
And without faith it is impossible to please God, because anyone who comes to him must believe that he exists and that he rewards those who earnestly seek him.

Prayer:

Thank You, Lord, for giving us the gift of faith. We understand that without it, it's impossible to please You. Your word declares that when we pray, we must believe that You exist and rewards the ones that earnestly seek You, in Jesus' name. Amen.

"Write out your prayer pertaining to the above scripture." _____
_____
_____
_____
_____

44. Intercessors hate what God hates

Scripture: Psalm 97:10 (NIV)
Let those who love the LORD hate evil, for he guards the lives of his faithful ones and delivers them from the hand of the wicked.

Prayer:

Thank You, Lord God, Your word declares that those who love You should hate evil, and because we hate what You hate, You will deliver us from the hand of the wicked, in Jesus' name. Amen.

"Write out your prayer pertaining to the above scripture." _____

_____
_____
_____
_____
_____
_____
_____

45. Intercessors obey God

Scripture: 1 Samuel 15:22 (NIV)

But Samuel replied:

> *"Does the LORD delight in burnt offerings and sacrifices as much as in obeying the LORD? To obey is better than sacrifice, and to heed is better than the fat of rams.*

Prayer:

Thank You, Lord, for imparting in me an obedient spirit, understanding that you would rather I obey You than to obey man. Because of Jesus Christ, I no longer have to sacrifice animals but surrender my body a living sacrifice, in Jesus' name. Amen.

"Write out your prayer pertaining to the above scripture." _____

_____

_____

_____

46. Intercessors make declarations

Scripture: Job 22:28 (KJV)
Thou shalt also decree a thing, and it shall be established unto thee: and the light shall shine upon thy ways.

Prayer:

Thank You, Lord that what I decree in the earth You will establish it unto me. God, I decree that my bloodlines are all saved, serving You the true and living God, in Jesus, name. Amen.

"Write out your prayer pertaining to the above scripture." _____

_____
_____
_____
_____
_____
_____
_____

47. Intercessors destroy the plans of hell

Scripture: Isaiah 59:19 (KJV)

So shall they fear the name of the LORD from the west, and his glory from the rising of the sun. When the enemy shall come in like a flood, the Spirit of the LORD shall lift up a standard against him.

Prayer:

Thank You, God, for Your power to destroy the plans of hell against my life and the life of my bloodline. Because of Your great name and power, people will fear and revere You, in Jesus' name. Amen.

"Write out your prayer pertaining to the above scripture." _____
_____
_____
_____
_____

48. Intercessors have access to heaven

Scripture: Revelations 5:8 (NASB)
When He had taken the book, the four living creatures and the twenty-four elders fell down before the Lamb, each one holding a harp and golden bowls full of incense, which are the prayers of the saints.

Prayer:

Thank You, Lord, for not only giving me access to the throne of Heaven but allowing my prayers to be answered. You hear and receive the prayers of the saints, in Jesus' name. Amen.

"Write out your prayer pertaining to the above scripture." _____
_____
_____
_____
_____
_____

49. Intercessors rebuke and correct

Scripture: Hebrews 12:6 (NIV)
because the Lord disciplines the one he loves, and he chastens everyone he accepts as his son."

Prayer:

Thank You, Lord God, for loving and correcting me. Because of your expression of love towards me, I can now live. Most of all, God, thank You for accepting me as Your child, in Jesus name. Amen.

"Write out your prayer pertaining to the above scripture." _____

_____
_____
_____
_____
_____
_____
_____

50. Intercessors are submissive

Scripture: Hebrews 13:17 (NIV)
Have confidence in your leaders and submit to their authority, because they keep watch over you as those who must give an account. Do this so that their work will be a joy, not a burden, for that would be of no benefit to you.

Prayer:

Thank You, Lord, for my leaders and those in authority You have placed over me. Bless them Father and give them the strength they need to continue to keep watch over me as they have to give an account to You, God. Let me be a blessing to my leaders and not a burden that I may bring joy to their hearts for all the hard work that they do, in the Name of Yeshua. Amen.

"Write out your prayer pertaining to the above scripture." _____

THE LIFE OF AN INTERCESSOR

Standing On The Power of Prayer

Tiffany Thompson has dedicated her life to prayer. She realized years ago that without prayer, you are on your own. Prayer goes before everything. When you need a sense of direction and guidance, you pray. When you have lost everything and trying to regain your life back, you pray. When you are under the weather, you pray. When life circumstances seem overwhelming, you pray. When you are looking for increase in every area of your life, you pray. Prayer is always in order.

Prayer helps develop a personal relationship with God. He enjoys talking to His children. Just imagine when you have no one to talk to and everyone is trying to do everything on their own not realizing that we have an advocate to stand in the gap for us. We have a right to go to the throne room and obtain mercy at a time of trouble.

ADDITIONAL DEDICATIONS

INTERCESSORS

The reason I placed the Intercessors first is because the office off an Intercessor is not an easy one. If you are one who has a plan/future, then you understand that everything is birthed out through intercession. It can be a church, a home, a child, a book, your marriage, calling, or a promise, it has to be taken to God in prayer. We have to war over whatever God promised. Your promise can be healing or deliverance either way you have to pray it through until you see it then you have to pray for it to reach full maturation.

The very first person, I have ever heard call on God in prayer is of course my mother Margie Thompson.

She may have not have called on Him in a way that I would actually know her relationship with God because we were not church goers as children, but it did not mean she did not know Him nor had a personal relationship with

Him. Honestly, the life I lived was more dangerous than some of the men I know and someone had to be praying in order for me to dodge death numerous times the way I did. So Yes! Big ups to my mother my first intercessor even when I had no clue of what an Intercessor was. I love you to pieces mom, thank you for not giving up on me.

The very next person I heard call on God was my grandmother, Mae Ivy Thompson. May her soul R.I.H.

She was my paternal grandmother and, my God, was she a praying woman. Her prayers were a little different from my mom's because this powerful woman called on God 24/7. I used to think as a kid *Grandma, it cannot be that bad. You are always calling on God, watching church on television, and going to church almost every day.* I am thinking *my mama do not do all of this, actually no one I have ever met does this.* I would ask her why do you have to go to church every day.

Well, grandma! You tried to tell me and now I have a clear understanding of why we have to always run to the throne of grace asking for forgiveness all day. Because when we seek God for real, He shows us all the ugliness that is inside of us and that is enough to keep us humble.

But most of all, this lady had a love for people that was unbelievable. If she could feed the entire neighborhood, she would, considering she had over ten children herself. She had my heart I was glued to her when we would visit.

She would never tell me, no, about anything. She served me my first cup of coffee when I was a kid. On the other hand, she made me taste a carrot for first time because she knew they were good for my eyes, I hated them!

I am sharing this with you because I am describing what the love of God looks like. She never whipped me nor was I called any ungodly name. I probably should have gotten disciplined because while she was getting dressed for church, I would run out the door and run up the road. I refused to sit in the church all those hours while the other children were outside playing.

Missing you Grandma!

This very next dedication goes to my very first spiritual mom ever and she is Missionary Mother Katherine Bynum.

I met her at a small church on the west side of Chicago through a sister in Christ holding prayer every Tuesday morning. **(I mentioned my experience at this church in the Introduction of this book.)** At the time, I was there thinking that I was giving my friend a ride to church, but yet I was being blessed. I ended up joining the church and remained there for a little over three years.

God allowed me to be a witness of how she loved, prayed, poured out, taught and trained the people of God. I thought to myself *who love's like this? This lady is phenomenal and where did she come from?* If you ever had a chance to meet her, you would know exactly what I am talking about. She is so genuine and you knew that she truly wanted you to be saved.

My impartation for Intercessory prayer first came from her. It reminds me of a Bible story when Paul told Timothy in 1 Timothy 4:14 (NIV), "Do not neglect your gift, which was given you through prophecy when the body of elders laid their hands on you."

She played a huge role in my life as she helped birth the Intercessor in me. Mother Katherine Bynum is a BLUEPRINT to follow, and still today, she is my spiritual mother.

This dedication right here is for my children because only God knows how to get everything that you have learned throughout the years and put it to great use.

My Sons are the first to receive this impartation, but I had to use everything I learned to go to war for them. These are the kings that God had come through my womb. The place of safety, the place that was an incubator for them to receive the nutrients they needed to be the men that they are becoming today. So know that you are not just in training or learning just to learn, there comes a time when you're going to have to apply all the tools, which is the word of faith, scripture, love, patience, boldness, confidence, power, etc. combined and go to war for your loved ones and God's people.

This last but not least dedication goes to my Apostles Dr. Matthew L. and Kamilah Stevenson lll.

I joined this ministry in the year 2012. I came in wounded and pretty much done with life, ministry, and everything. But because of their prayers and supplications toward me, and their obedience to God, I am still here today going strong.

My Apostles held all kinds of classes on Intercession, Prayer, warfare, etc. to instruct me and build me up. They have even brought in great people who carry the mantle of Intercession on them to bless the people of God. I see them as people who see the need and the burden to help everyone through the operation of Holy Spirit.

I thank the Lord for the grace that is on their lives and what is in the house. Because of these classes and trainings, it taught me patience, perseverance, love, and how to not just pray, but how to effectively pray using scripture and not just speaking in tongues. My prayer life has been elevated to pray with power, confidence, boldness, assurance, strength and faith.

What had happened, everything I learned or thought I knew throughout the years of being trained in different areas by many generals were all put in a great big bowl, blended together, and put in proper order. Now, it all makes sense. God was making an Intercessor out of me all along.

By:

Born with Purpose

A life story that shares Tiffany's experiences from the time she was a little girl.

www.ingramcontent.com/pod-product-compliance
Lightning Source LLC
Chambersburg PA
CBHW070549300426
44113CB00011B/1841